How To ~~Pass~~ BLITZ.
ABRSM Theory
Grade 3

by Samantha Coates

Published by
Chester Music,
part of The Music Sales Group,
14-15 Berners Street,
London W1T 3LJ, UK.

Exclusive Distributors:
Music Sales Limited
Distribution Centre, Newmarket Road,
Bury St Edmunds, Suffolk IP33 3YB, UK.

Music Sales Pty Limited
4th floor, Lisgar House,
30-32 Carrington Street,
Sydney, NSW 2000, Australia.

Order No. CH85173
ISBN 978-1-78558-356-8

Printed in the EU.

Your Guarantee of Quality:

As publishers, we strive to produce every book
to the highest commercial standards.

Particular care has been given to specifying acid-free, neutral-sized
paper made from pulps which have not been elemental chlorine bleached.

This pulp is from farmed sustainable forests and was
produced with special regard for the environment.

Throughout, the printing and binding have been planned to ensure
a sturdy, attractive publication which should give years of enjoyment.

If your copy fails to meet our high standards,
please inform us and we will gladly replace it.

www.musicsales.com

A Note From the Author

←——————————————————→

Dear theory student,

Congratulations! You have just done the very best thing for your theory education — you've bought this book.

This Grade 3 Theory book contains more information, more revision and more worksheets than any other theory text book (except maybe How To Blitz ABRSM Theory Grades 1 and 2!).

This book follows on from the knowledge you gained in Grade 2. If you have skipped Grades 1 and 2 and you are 'jumping in' at Grade 3 level, there may be some things you need to brush up on. It's actually a great idea to work through the workbooks from previous grades before you start this book, but you should discuss this with your teacher.

Every time you see this icon: it means there are extra resources available on the website.

Go to www.blitzbooks.com to download free worksheets, flashcards, manuscript and more!

Happy theory—ing,

Samantha

It takes more than an author and a publisher to produce a book — it takes enormous support from friends and family. Thank you to everyone who has helped me on the BlitzBooks journey, but most of all to Andrew, Thomas and Courtney... without you three, there would simply be no books.

Contents

Remembering Relatives

Related keys share the same key signature. You can work out the relative minor of any major key by 'counting' down three semitones on a keyboard. In Grade 2 we learned that the best way to remember relatives is to make up a word beginning and ending with the letters of the related keys!

Relatives	Key Signature of These Keys	Word to Remember Relatives
C major is related to **A minor**		word beginning with 'C' and ending with 'A': _____
G major is related to **E minor**		word beginning with 'G' and ending with 'E': _____
F major is related to **D minor**		word beginning with 'F' and ending with 'D': _____
D major is related to **B minor** new!		word beginning with 'D' and ending with 'B': _____

Write these key signatures (watch out for clef changes!):

D major   B minor   D minor   F major   B minor

E Major and the Sharps

E major is one of our new sharp keys in Grade 3. Now we know four major keys with sharps:

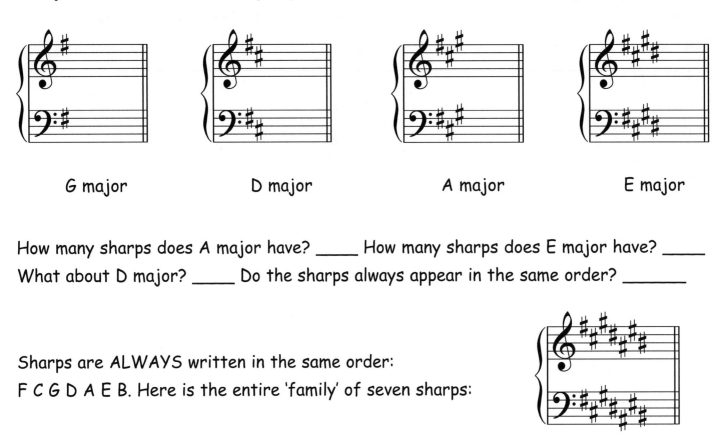

| G major | D major | A major | E major |

How many sharps does A major have? _____ How many sharps does E major have? _____
What about D major? _____ Do the sharps always appear in the same order? _____

Sharps are ALWAYS written in the same order:
F C G D A E B. Here is the entire 'family' of seven sharps:

There is an easy way to remember this order. You just need a sentence where the beginning of each word tells you the name of the sharp, for instance:

<u>F</u>at <u>C</u>at <u>G</u>oes <u>D</u>riving <u>A</u>nd <u>E</u>ats <u>B</u>ananas'

Try making up your own sentence here! (Go to www.blitzbooks.com for some great 'sentence' ideas!)

F_____   C_____   G_____   D_____   A_____   E_____   B_____

Apart from getting the order of sharps right, it's important to write them in exactly the right position every time. Write these key signatures (watch out for clef changes!):

| E major | D major | A major | E major | G major |

6

Minor Sharp Keys

In Grade 3 we have to learn about minor keys with up to **four** sharps. Here they are:

E minor   B minor   F♯ minor   C♯ minor

Write the following key signatures:

C♯ minor   B minor   E minor   F♯ minor

Name these MINOR key signatures:

_____   _____   _____   _____   _____

And now name these MAJOR key signatures!

_____   _____   _____   _____   _____

Name the two keys that share this key signature:

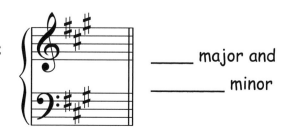

_____ major and

_____ minor

Major Flat Keys

The new flat key in Grade 3 is A♭ major. So now you know four major keys with flats:

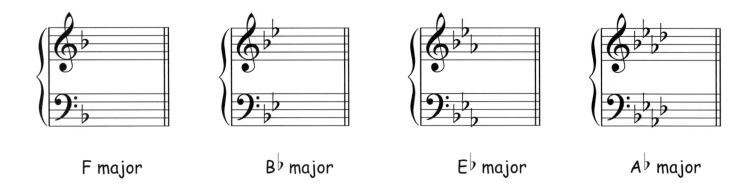

F major   B♭ major   E♭ major   A♭ major

How many flats does E♭ major have? _____ How many flats in A♭ major? _____What about
B♭ major? _____ Do the flats always appear in the same order? _____

Flats also are ALWAYS written in the same order:
B E A D G C F. Here is the entire 'family' of flats:

You might be thinking we need to make up another sentence for the order of flats. Well
guess what? We don't have to... it's the same as the order of the sharps, but BACKWARDS!
(How convenient)

We also need to get the positioning of the flats just right. Write these key signatures (watch
out for clef changes!):

B♭ major   A♭ major   E♭ major   E♭ major   A♭ major

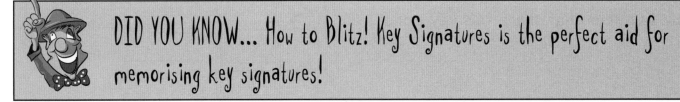

DID YOU KNOW... How to Blitz! Key Signatures is the perfect aid for memorising key signatures!

8

Minor Flat Keys

As we discussed on page 5, relative major and minor keys share the same key signature. Look at the key signatures on the opposite page, then complete these sentences:

G minor is the relative of
B♭ major, therefore it
has _____ flats.

C minor is the relative of
E♭ major, therefore it
has _____ flats.

F minor is the relative of
A♭ major, therefore it
has _____ flats.

G minor

C minor

F minor

Write the key signatures on the staves above, and memorise them!

Can you add accidentals to make this a G harmonic minor scale? Don't forget you'll need the flats that are in the key signature PLUS you must raise the 7th note!

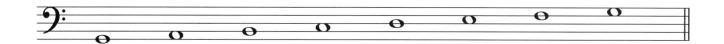

Good work! Now, C and F harmonic minor are just a teensy bit tricky, since the 7th note is affected by the key signature. We must use a NATURAL sign to raise it!

Here is C harmonic minor:

See? The 7th note was a B♭ but now it is raised to a B♮

Can you try writing an F harmonic minor scale? Use semibreves and write one octave ascending. Remember to raise the 7th note (hint: you won't be using a sharp sign to do it!).

Let's Write Scales

Top Tips for Superb Scales

🚩 You may be asked to write scales with key signatures OR accidentals – read the question carefully!

🚩 You have to know how to write **two** types of minor scales: harmonic and melodic

🚩 Remember to **raise the 7th note** in harmonic minor (going up and down)

🚩 Remember to **raise the 6th AND 7th notes** in melodic minor (going up)

🚩 Remember to **LOWER the 6th and 7th notes** in melodic minor (going down)

🚩 Scale writing in Grade 3 is easy as long as you have revised all your Grade 2 stuff!

1. Write an F♯ melodic minor scale:

★ write the key signature

★ use semibreves

★ write one octave ascending

2. Write a B harmonic minor scale:

★ use accidentals

★ use crotchets

★ write one octave going down

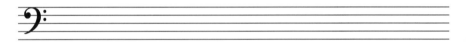

3. Write the minor scale (either harmonic or melodic) with the given key signature:

★ use minims

★ write one octave going up

Which form have you chosen to write? _____

4. Add a clef and any accidentals required to make this an A♭ major scale.

5. Continue the melodic minor scale beginning on this note:

★ do not write the key signature, use accidentals instead

★ write one octave going up and back down again

★ remember to raise/lower notes with the correct accidentals

6. Write a C harmonic minor scale:

★ write the key signature

★ use crotchets

★ write two octaves descending (double the fun!)

WARNING: Super-challenging question coming up!

7. Using the treble clef, write the major scale with four sharps:

★ do not write the key signature, use accidentals

★ use semibreves

★ write two octaves going up

★ mark the semitones in the lower octave

★ complete the scale with a double bar-line

8. Name this scale:

Go to **www.blitzbooks.com** and download the 'Scale Mania' page for more practice on writing scales!

Tonic Triads

Writing tonic triads in Grade 3 is almost as easy as it was in Grades 1 and 2... you just need to know all your new key signatures!

1. Write these tonic triads, each with a key signature. Watch out for clef changes!

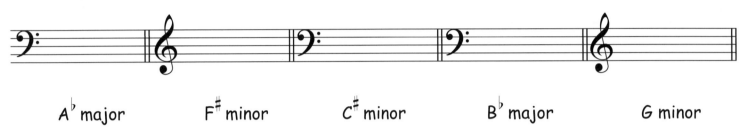

A♭ major   F♯ minor   C♯ minor   B♭ major   G minor

2. Write the tonic triads for these MINOR key signatures:

3. Name these tonic triads. Remember, check the bottom note and the accidentals!

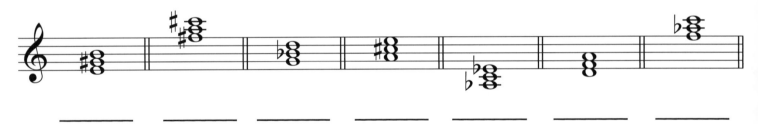

_____   _____   _____   _____   _____   _____

4. Add a clef and any necessary accidentals to make these tonic triads correct.

E major   F minor   A♭ major   F♯ minor   C♯ minor

5. Which triad is made up of the notes B, D, F♯ ? _____

6. Name the notes contained in an E♭ major tonic triad: _____ _____ _____

Tiny Test

1. Write an F melodic minor scale, one octave ascending, using semibreves, with a key signature.

2. Add a clef and the correct key signature to each of these tonic triads.

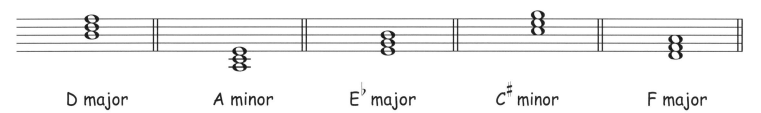

D major   A minor   E♭ major   C♯ minor   F major

3. Which two keys share this key signature?

_____ and _____

4. Here is a rather incomplete melody. Follow the instructions below!

★ Add the correct clef and key signature to make it a melody in C minor.

★ At each place marked with an asterisk, add one note from the C minor tonic triad (use crotchets). (Use a different note on each beat!)

★ Find all the 7th scale degrees and raise them by a semitone.

★ Add the missing bar-lines.

★ Circle the shortest note in the melody.

Total:

Demisemiquavers (a.k.a. super-short notes)

Remember semiquavers? They have two tails like this: ♪ (or two beams like this: ♫) and they are worth a quarter of a beat each. That makes them rather short.

But there's a shorter note... a demisemiquaver! ♪ (or ♫) Demisemiquavers have THREE tails (or three beams) which makes them half as long as a semiquaver. So they are worth $\frac{1}{8}$ of a crotchet beat each.

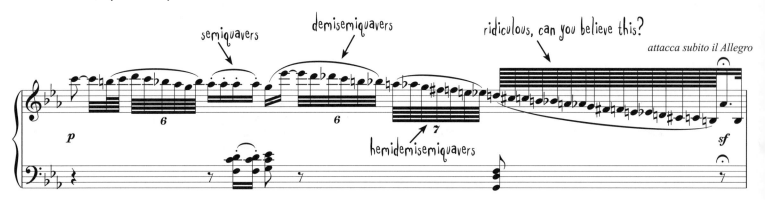

The reason we need to know about demisemiquavers is because a) we find them in music, like in this piece by Beethoven:

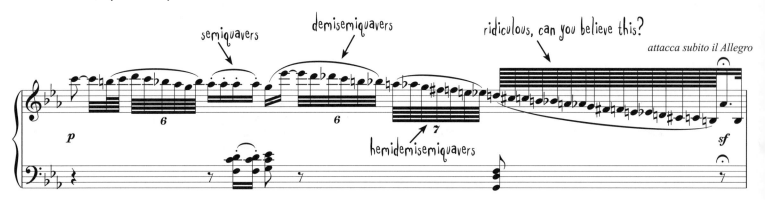

and b) you MUST use one straight after a dotted semiquaver.

So ♪. ($\frac{3}{8}$ of a beat) must be followed by ♪ ($\frac{1}{8}$ of a beat) which becomes ♫ !

You can also have a demisemiquaver rest. You guessed it... this rest has THREE hooks: 𝄿

Which of these groups of notes are equal to one quaver beat? Circle them.

Now put a square around the remaining groups. They are each worth a _____ beat.

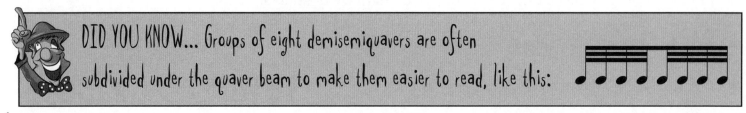

DID YOU KNOW... Groups of eight demisemiquavers are often subdivided under the quaver beam to make them easier to read, like this:

14

Rhythm Things

Quick revision of time signatures we know from Grade 2: $\frac{2}{4}$, $\frac{3}{4}$, $\frac{4}{4}$, $\frac{2}{2}$, $\frac{3}{2}$, $\frac{4}{2}$, $\frac{3}{8}$ (quite a few, eh?)

1. Add the correct time signature to these one-bar rhythms featuring demisemiquavers:

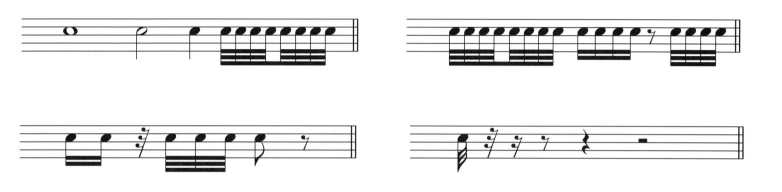

2. Add the missing bar-lines to these melodies (which, once again, feature demisemiquavers):

3. At each place marked *, add the missing rest or rests:

4. How many demisemiquavers are there in a dotted semibreve? (Hint: LOTS) _____

5. Fill this bar with demisemiquavers:

The Anacrusis (a.k.a. 'upbeat')

The formal definition of an anacrusis, or 'upbeat', is 'one or more unaccented notes before the first bar-line'. Here are some rather famous examples of tunes with an anacrusis:

Hap - py BIRTH-day to you, Hap - py birth - day to you

We WISH you a mer-ry Christ-mas, we wish you a mer-ry Christ-mas

When you sing these, notice how the anacrusis is not accented.
It is the first beat of the first bar that is accented.

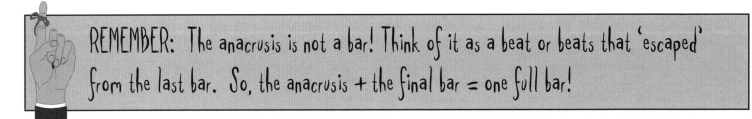

REMEMBER: The anacrusis is not a bar! Think of it as a beat or beats that 'escaped' from the last bar. So, the anacrusis + the final bar = one full bar!

The following rhythms begin with an upbeat, but the last bar in each is WRONG – it does not allow for the upbeat. Can you rewrite each rhythm with the correct final bar?

See? This allows for the upbeat

16

More Rhythm Things

1. These melodies each begin with an upbeat. Can you figure out where the bar-lines go?

2. Compose the final bar of this rhythm. Remember to allow for the anacrusis!

3. Write a suitable upbeat for each of these rhythms:

4. Rewrite these notes/rests in the correct order, from **shortest** to **longest**.

5. Add the correct time signature to this melody. When you are counting the beats in each bar, rememeber this: the upbeat + the last bar = one full bar!

Halving and Doubling

In Grade 2 you learned how to rewrite a melody with all the note values either halved or doubled. It's just the same in Grade 3... except the new time signature is not given to you – you have to figure it out yourself! (That's the down side of getting older)

When you halve or double the note values, you are changing the **bottom** number of the time signature. The top number DOES NOT CHANGE. Here's the rule:

Notes **doubled** = bottom number **halved**

Notes **halved** = bottom number **doubled**

Complete this table:

Time signature	Notes doubled (bottom number halved)	Notes halved (bottom number doubled)
$\frac{2}{4}$	$\frac{2}{2}$	
$\frac{3}{4}$		$\frac{3}{8}$
$\frac{4}{4}$		
$\frac{2}{2}$		
$\frac{3}{2}$		
$\frac{4}{2}$		
$\frac{3}{8}$		

The reason some of the boxes are greyed out is that we don't study time signatures like 2/8 and 3/16!!!

Ok, here we go! Rewrite the melodies below with notes TWICE the value (i.e. doubled). (Quick reminder of our Grade 2 strategy: write the new note values above the original melody, then you can see how they should be grouped.)

Insert new time signature!

18

And now rewrite these melodies, with notes and rests of HALF the value. As usual, the key signature is given to you, but you have to write the new time signature.

Here's an interesting one... first, add the missing rest/s where you see *. Then rewrite the whole melody with notes and rests of **twice** the value.

Don't get tricked! Check the opening!

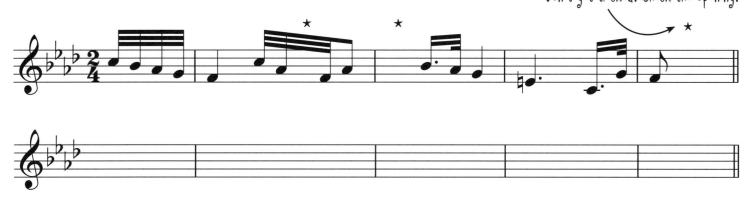

And for your final trick... add the correct clef, key signature AND time signature to this melody in F♯ minor. Then rewrite on the staff below with notes of **half** the value. You'll need to write the clef and key signature again, as well as the new time signature!

HOT TIP: If you double all the notes of a melody in $\frac{2}{4}$, you end up with $\frac{2}{2}$, not $\frac{4}{4}$!

Meet $\frac{6}{8}$ Time

Up until now we've only had time signatures with the number 2, 3 or 4 on the top. These were all 'simple' time signatures.

Well, $\frac{6}{8}$ is a 'compound' time signature. It's so different, it's as if it's from MARS!

The '6' on the top means that there are six beats in the bar, and the '8' on the bottom means that the beats are quaver beats. BUT... the proper definition of $\frac{6}{8}$ is NOT 'six quavers per bar'! (Contrary to popular opinion)

Let's compare the time signature of $\frac{3}{4}$. It also has six quavers per bar:

   This grouping shows us **three crotchet** beats.

But $\frac{6}{8}$, which also has six quavers per bar, is very different because...
THE QUAVERS ARE GROUPED IN THREES! (Incredibly important)

In $\frac{6}{8}$, a bar full of quavers looks like this:

   This grouping shows us **two dotted crotchet** beats.

So when we are describing $\frac{6}{8}$, it's not enough to say 'six quavers per bar' because that does not tell us anything about the way the quavers are grouped. We have to say **'two dotted crotchets per bar'**.

$\frac{3}{4}$ versus $\frac{6}{8}$	$\frac{3}{4}$ Simple Triple	$\frac{6}{8}$ Compound Duple
Grouping of Quavers	♫ ♫ ♫	♫♫ ♫♫
Beats Shown	♩ ♩ ♩	♩. ♩.

'Compound' time means dotted beats. In $\frac{6}{8}$ there are two dotted-crotchet beats per bar. This means the definition of $\frac{6}{8}$ is **'compound duple'**.

$\frac{6}{8}$ is From Mars

As we discussed on the previous page, $\frac{6}{8}$ is incredibly different to the other time signatures we've studied. The grouping is all different, and we have to switch our thinking...

Grouping Rules	Simple (Earth) Plain, Undotted beats	Compound (Mars) Dotted Beats
Groups of Quavers	In simple time, i.e. on Earth, quavers are grouped in TWOS and FOURS.	$\frac{6}{8}$ comes from Mars. It looks completely different because the quavers are grouped in THREES.
Dotted Crotchet	On Earth, ♩. is worth 1½ beats. ♩. must be followed by ♪ (or equivalent) On Earth, 𝄽. is not allowed.	On Mars, ♩. does NOT mean 1½ beats. On Mars, ♩. = 1 whole beat. On Mars, 𝄽. is allowed, it is 1 beat.
Plain Crotchet	On Earth, a plain crotchet is one whole beat.	On Mars, a plain crotchet is NOT a whole beat. ♩ must be followed by ♪ or 𝄾 (or equivalent, such as ♫♫ !)
Minims	Minims and minim rests are very common on Earth. They may occur at the beginning or halfway through the bar.	Minims and minim rests are FORBIDDEN on Mars!

'Simple' means plain, undotted beats. 'Compound' means dotted beats.

Grouping in $\frac{6}{8}$

Rhythms in $\frac{6}{8}$ must be clearly divided into two halves. Draw a dotted line down the middle of each of the bars below, i.e. you need three quaver beats on each side (the first is done for you):

Notice how rests and groups of notes never cross the dotted line? This is because in $\frac{6}{8}$, in fact in all compound time signatures (we're learning more later on, yay!), each dotted-crotchet beat needs its own group of notes or rests. If notes or rests cross the dotted line, it's wrong!

Be very careful with crotchet rests in $\frac{6}{8}$. They may ONLY fall at the beginning of a group of three quaver beats. So, ♪ 𝄽 is not allowed. It needs to be ♪ ♪ ♪

(For more info see 'Rests in Compound Time' on page 34)

Wrong ✗	Why is it Wrong?	Fix it Up! ✓
$\frac{6}{8}$ ♩. ♪ 𝄽	can't have crotchet rest on 2nd or 5th quaver beat	
$\frac{6}{8}$ ♫♫♫	quavers must be grouped in threes	
$\frac{6}{8}$ ▬ ♫	minim rest must be split to show dotted-crotchet beats	
$\frac{6}{8}$ ♪ 𝄽 ♪ ♪	single quaver must be followed by quaver rests	

Complete These Bars

On this page you'll need to complete the given bars in certain ways. You must be able to switch your thinking from 'Earth' to 'Mars' depending on which time signature you see!

Simple (Earth) – $\frac{2}{4}$, $\frac{3}{4}$, $\frac{4}{4}$ etc.	Compound (Mars) – $\frac{6}{8}$
★ make half beats up to whole beats ★ quavers are grouped in twos/fours ★ dotted-crotchet rests don't exist	★ dotted beats ARE whole beats ★ quavers are grouped in threes ★ minim rests don't exist here

1. Complete these bars using a rest or rests in the correct order. Double check the time signature to know which planet you are on!

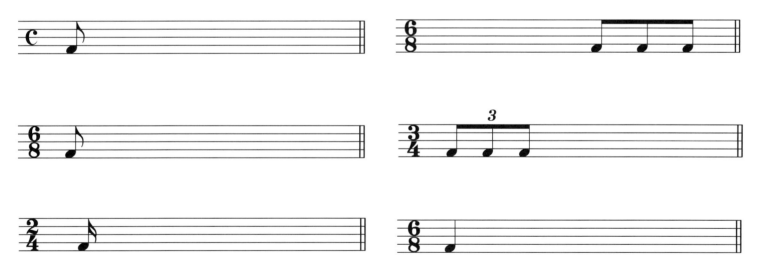

2. At each place marked with an asterisk, add the correct rest or rests.

Did you see the anacrusis? Check your final bar carefully!

3. Complete these bars with quavers correctly grouped.

Quick Quiz

1. Add the correct time signatures to these melodies:

2. State whether these time signatures are simple or compound, and then whether they are duple, triple or quadruple. (This is a very formal way of saying 'explain these time signatures in full'!)

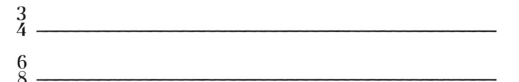

3. Add a time signature AND the missing bar-lines to this melody:

4. Rewrite the following melody with the notes correctly grouped/beamed.

Intervals

To name an interval in Grades 1 and 2, all we had to do was count up from the bottom note. But now we have to include more information than just the number. We must also name the 'type' of interval (oooaahh):

In Grade 3 there are three categories of 'type': **major**, **minor** and **perfect**.

Major scales contain intervals that are either **major** or **perfect**.

Harmonic minor scales contain all three types of intervals: **major**, **minor** and **perfect**.

IMPORTANT FACT: Minor intervals are one semitone smaller than major intervals.

Look at these harmonic intervals above the tonic of D. The top note of each interval comes from the D MAJOR scale:

perfect unison   major 2nd   **major** 3rd   perfect 4th   perfect 5th   **major** 6th   major 7th   perfect 8ve

Now look at these intervals. The top notes come from the D HARMONIC MINOR scale:

perfect unison   major 2nd   **minor** 3rd   perfect 4th   perfect 5th   **minor** 6th   major 7th   perfect 8ve

Things to Notice:

★ The 3rd and the 6th are the only two intervals that are different in the two sets.

★ The 2nd and 7th are 'major' intervals, even in the minor scale. More about this later!

Unisons, 4ths, 5ths and 8ves

Look back at the intervals on the previous page. The unisons, 4ths, 5ths and 8ves are the same in both scales. These are the 'perfect' intervals.

HOT TIP: Unisons, 4ths, 5ths and 8ves are exactly the same in major and minor scales, and they are always PERFECT. They are NEVER major or minor.

When naming intervals, always write the type **before** the number, e.g. 'perfect 4th', not '4th perfect'.

Name these harmonic intervals by number and type (remember, write 'perfect 5th', not '5th perfect'):

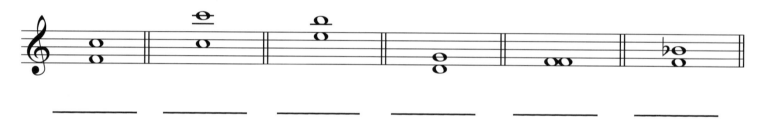

_____   _____   _____   _____   _____   _____

Sometimes you'll be asked to write the 'type' on a separate line. Fill in the type (e.g. perfect) and number (e.g. 5th) of each of the melodic intervals below:

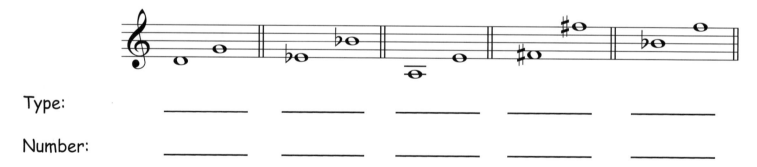

Type: _____   _____   _____   _____   _____   _____

Number: _____   _____   _____   _____   _____   _____

Can you write these harmonic intervals? They are all in the key of D major.

   perfect 5th   perfect unison   perfect 4th   perfect 8ve   perfect 5th

2nds and 7ths

2nds and 7ths are a bit tricky. They are MAJOR even in minor keys!

Minor 2nds do exist, but not in the scales we're studying at the moment. All harmonic minor scales contain major 2nds and 7ths.

HOT TIP: 2nds and 7ths are MAJOR, even in minor keys. The only exception is the 7th in a descending melodic minor scale. Discuss this more with your teacher!

Check out these harmonic intervals:

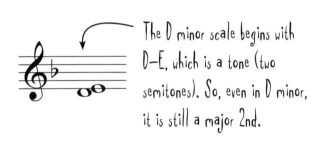

The D minor scale begins with D-E, which is a tone (two semitones). So, even in D minor, it is still a major 2nd.

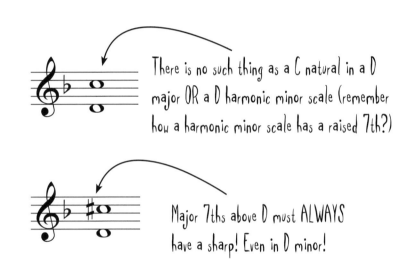

There is no such thing as a C natural in a D major OR a D harmonic minor scale (remember how a harmonic minor scale has a raised 7th?)

Major 7ths above D must ALWAYS have a sharp! Even in D minor!

Name these melodic intervals by type and number.

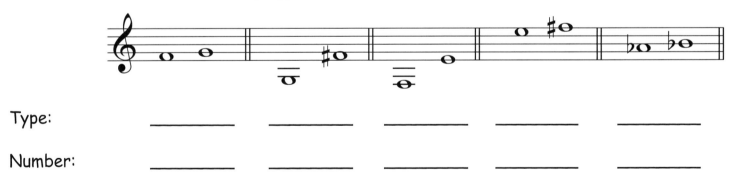

Type: _____   _____   _____   _____   _____

Number: _____   _____   _____   _____   _____

Write these harmonic intervals (i.e. directly above the given note) in the key of A♭ major:

major 7th   major 2nd   perfect 5th   perfect 4th   perfect 8ve   perfect unison

3rds and 6ths

⟷

> **HOT TIP:** 3rds and 6ths can be either MAJOR or MINOR. It depends on whether you're dealing with a major or minor key!

When you're trying to work out the 'type' of a 3rd or a 6th, use these three simple steps:

1. Look at the **key signature** and the **lower note** of the interval, to work out the key.

    (In fact you often won't even need this step, since you are usually told the key. Yippee!)

2. If the key is MAJOR, 3rds and 6ths will be MAJOR.

3. If the key is MINOR, 3rds and 6ths will be MINOR.

Name these harmonic intervals by type and number (remember, write 'major 6th', not '6th major'):

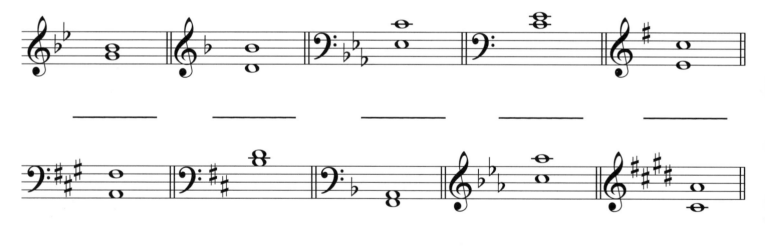

Describe these melodic intervals, which are all in the key of F minor. (Being told it's a minor key means you already know the 'type' of the 3rds and 6ths. Don't get tricked by the 2nds and 7ths!)

Writing Major 7ths

Writing major 7ths can be a little tricky, depending on the key. Here's the thing:

In **major** keys: no problem! Just count up seven notes from the tonic (including the tonic note as no. 1, of course) and you're done.

In **minor** keys: slight problem! You will often be asked to write a major 7th in a minor key, so you will have to RAISE it with an accidental! (Otherwise it will be marked wrong and that would be sad)

Most of the time, you'll raise the 7th with a sharp sign. But there are two exceptions:

C minor 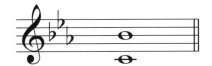   F minor

Which accidental will you need? Sharp/flat/natural (circle correct answer, then raise the 7ths above!)

Write major 7ths next to each of these tonic notes (i.e. write melodic intervals). All of the keys are MINOR, so you'll need accidentals!

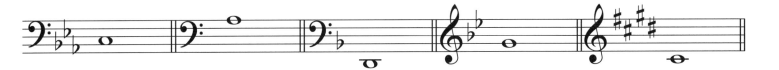

In the exercise below, not all of the keys are minor! Check the key signature and tonic note to work out the key, then write major 7ths **above** each note. Remember:

★ In **major** keys, major 7ths don't need anything.
★ In **minor** keys, major 7ths need to be raised with an accidental (which could be a sharp OR a natural).

HOT TIP: If you are asked to write a minor 7th in a minor key, you won't need an accidental. Minor 7ths are found in the descending melodic minor scale.

Let's Write Intervals

Quick Revision of Things We Know:

★ Unisons, 4ths, 5ths and 8ves are _____

★ 2nds and 7ths are almost always _____

★ 3rds and 6ths can be _____ or _____

Remember, the **lower** note of the interval is the tonic. Check out these D minor intervals:

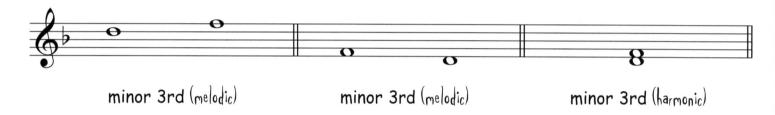

minor 3rd (melodic)   minor 3rd (melodic)   minor 3rd (harmonic)

Ok, here we go! For each of the following melodic intervals, name the key, type and number. Remember, the lower note is the tonic note in that key.

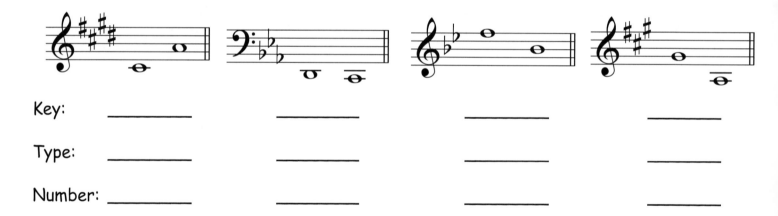

Key: _____   _____   _____   _____

Type: _____   _____   _____   _____

Number: _____   _____   _____   _____

Study this melody in C# minor, then circle all the intervals of a minor 3rd.

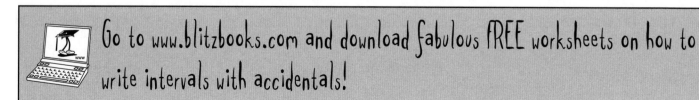

Go to www.blitzbooks.com and download fabulous FREE worksheets on how to write intervals with accidentals!

Extremely Short Test

1. Name the following scales. If they are minor, state which type of minor.

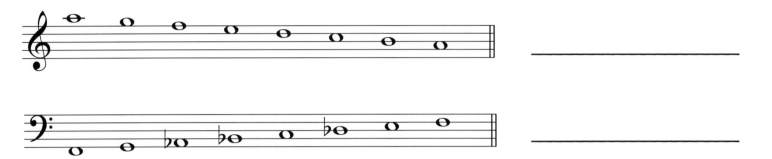

_____

_____

2. Fix the grouping in this short rhythm by beaming the notes correctly.

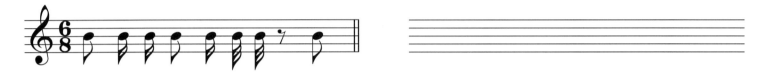

3. Name these intervals. They are all in the key of D major.

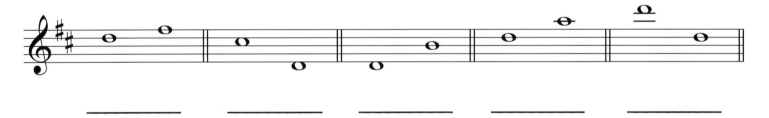

_____ _____ _____ _____ _____

4. Write the melodic minor scale that has this key signature. Write one octave ascending, and write the scale using minims.

5. Complete the following bars using only demisemiquavers. (This will take patience.)

$\frac{9}{8}$ is Just Like $\frac{6}{8}$

$\frac{9}{8}$ has nine quaver beats per bar, and the beats are grouped into threes. So $\frac{9}{8}$ means '**three dotted crotchets per bar, compound triple**'. It's also from Mars; it's like an extension of $\frac{6}{8}$!

Time Signature	Beats	Grouping of Quavers
$\frac{6}{8}$	♩. ♩.	♫♫♫ ♫♫♫
$\frac{9}{8}$	♩. ♩. ♩.	♫♫♫ ♫♫♫ ♫♫♫

Write the correct time signature for these rhythms:

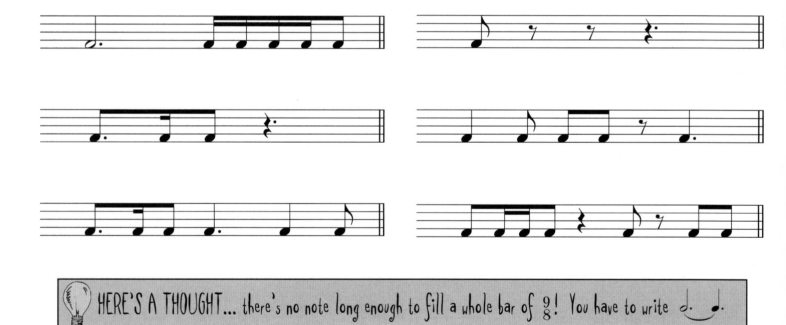

HERE'S A THOUGHT... there's no note long enough to fill a whole bar of $\frac{9}{8}$! You have to write ♩.͜♩.

Add the missing bar-lines to these melodies.

32

Introducing: $\frac{12}{8}$

$\frac{12}{8}$ is very similar to $\frac{6}{8}$ and $\frac{9}{8}$, which we have just studied (how convenient). It is also from Mars. $\frac{12}{8}$ simply has one extra dotted-crotchet beat in the bar!

Time Sig.	Beats	Grouping of Quavers	Definition
$\frac{6}{8}$	♩. ♩.	♫♫ ♫♫	compound duple
$\frac{9}{8}$	♩. ♩. ♩.	♫♫ ♫♫ ♫♫	compound triple
$\frac{12}{8}$	♩. ♩. ♩. ♩.	♫♫ ♫♫ ♫♫ ♫♫	compound quadruple

DID YOU KNOW... A dotted-minim rest like this: ▬· fills up half a bar in $\frac{12}{8}$ time!

The grouping rules are the same in all compound time signatures. Make sure all notes and rests are grouped in threes, so that they clearly show the dotted-crotchet beats.

Complete the following bars with **quavers** correctly grouped:

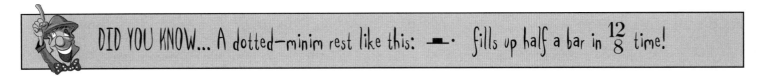

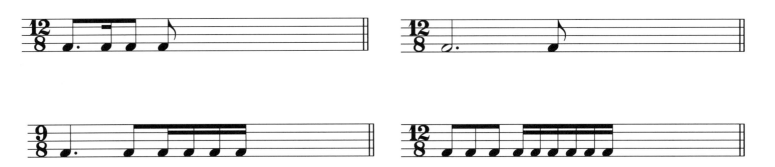

Insert the correct time signatures for these one-bar rhythms:

Rests in Compound Time

Like notes, rests must also be grouped to show dotted-crotchet beats in compound time. Look at the difference between $\frac{6}{8}$ and $\frac{3}{4}$, when both bars start with crotchets:

In compound time, a dotted crotchet's worth of silence can be written two ways:

It should not be written like this 𝄾 𝄾 𝄾 and NEVER like this 𝄾 𝄽

As discussed back on page 22, a crotchet rest may NOT occur on the second of three quaver beats. For example, it is not ok to write ♪ 𝄽 ! This is incorrect grouping. The crotchet rest must be split into two quavers like this: ♪ 𝄾 𝄾

When checking your grouping, it really helps if you draw dotted lines dividing the bars into dotted crotchet beats. Here is an example of grouping in $\frac{9}{8}$ time, first wrong, then right!

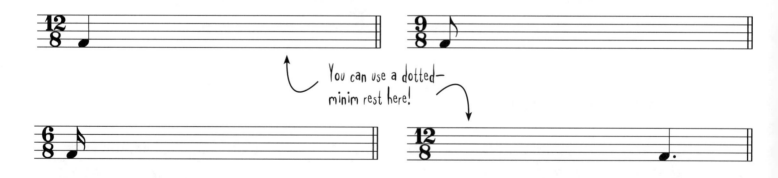

Complete these bars with rests. Make sure your grouping shows compound time.

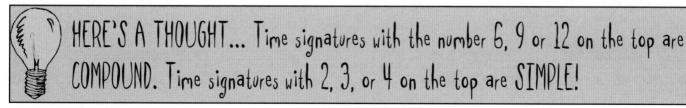

You can use a dotted-minim rest here!

Definitions of Time Signatures

The full definition of a time signature should include the number and type of beats in each bar, as well as stating whether it is simple or compound, and whether it is duple, triple or quadruple time. Here is an example of a perfect conversation with an examiner:

Examiner: 'What does $\frac{6}{8}$ mean?'

You: 'It means two dotted crotchets per bar, compound duple.'

Examiner: 'High Distinction for you.'

Complete this table and you'll be super-prepared to define all of these time signatures!

Time Signature	Description	Simple or Compound?	Duple, Triple, or Quadruple?
$\frac{6}{8}$	two dotted crotchets per bar	compound	duple
$\frac{2}{2}$ or ¢			
$\frac{4}{4}$ or C			
$\frac{9}{8}$			
$\frac{3}{8}$			
$\frac{2}{4}$			
$\frac{3}{4}$			
$\frac{4}{2}$			
$\frac{12}{8}$			
$\frac{3}{2}$			

Box Puzzle

←——————→

Fill in the answers to the clues below, and find the secret message running down the page... it's what you have to do to certain intervals in minor keys!

1. One or more unaccented beats before the first bar-line
2. The full definition of $\frac{4}{2}$ is four minims in a bar, _____ _____ (two words)
3. Note worth $\frac{1}{8}$ of a crotchet beat
4. In melodic minor scales, the 7th note is always _____ on the way up
5. In melodic minor scales, the 7th note is always _____ on the way down
6. Unisons, 4ths, 5ths and 8ves are _____
7. The key signature of C$\sharp$ minor contains _____ _____ (two words)
8. $\frac{6}{8}$ is an example of compound _____ time
9. Italian term meaning moderately short and detached (you learned this in Grade 2!)
10. There are two of these per bar in compound-duple time
11. Another name for a whole-bar rest
12. These intervals are major in harmonic minor scales and minor in the descending melodic minor (how complicated!)
13. Another name for a semitone (hint: smaller than a major second)
14. Major key with four flats
15. Number of demisemiquavers in a minim tied to a semiquaver

Add Bar-lines

Add bar-lines to each of these melodies (some have an upbeat). Remember your grouping rules:

★ In compound time – $\frac{6}{8}$, $\frac{9}{8}$ and $\frac{12}{8}$ – quavers are grouped in **threes** (or sometimes sixes, for semiquavers!). Think MARS.

★ In simple time, quavers are grouped in **twos** and **fours**. Think EARTH.

What's the Time?

Figuring out the correct time signature of a melody can be tricky, now that we're dealing with simple AND compound time.

When you are asked to identify the time signature, don't just start counting up beats. First look over the **whole** melody. Think to yourself: is it simple-ish, or compound-ish? (Is it from Earth, or Mars?) What clues can I see that give this away?

This first bar is awfully complicated, let's ignore it for now

Here is a BIG clue – a dotted crotchet rest! These don't exist in simple time

These quavers are grouped in threes – must be compound time

All the clues above point to compound time (Mars!). This means there are only three options for the time signature: $\frac{6}{8}$, $\frac{9}{8}$ or $\frac{12}{8}$. Insert the correct one now!

Insert the correct time signature for each of the next 11 (yes, 11!) melodies. Some of them begin on an upbeat – remember that this is not a bar! Start by looking over the whole melody and thinking: is it simple-ish or compound-ish?

Compose a Rhythm

In Grade 2 you learned to compose a four-bar rhythm based on a given opening. Well, in Grade 3 you have to do exactly the same thing! There are just two important differences:

1. The given opening might be incomplete. You will have to complete it before moving on.

2. The opening may begin on an upbeat. This means you'll have to adjust your final bar.

In fact, it's quite possible that your opening will be incomplete AND have an anacrusis (whoa)!

In Grade 2 we also learned some strategies for composing a four-bar rhythm. Here they are again (keeping in mind that your given opening is represented by the symbol △):

	Bar 1	Bar 2	Bar 3	Bar 4
Option 1	△	something super creative	repeat △	long note
Option 2	△	△ with some changes	△ with even more changes	long note
Option 3	△	contrasting idea	something similar to △	long note

Now that you're in Grade 3, you should probably experiment with a little more interest in your final bar – try doing something creative for the first half of the bar, and then using longer note values in the second half.

Here are a whole bunch of openings, some with an anacrusis, some incomplete, some both!

Remember to observe the time signature, count up the beats given and adjust your final bar if necessary.

And the most important thing of all... CLAP your rhythm to yourself and to your teacher!

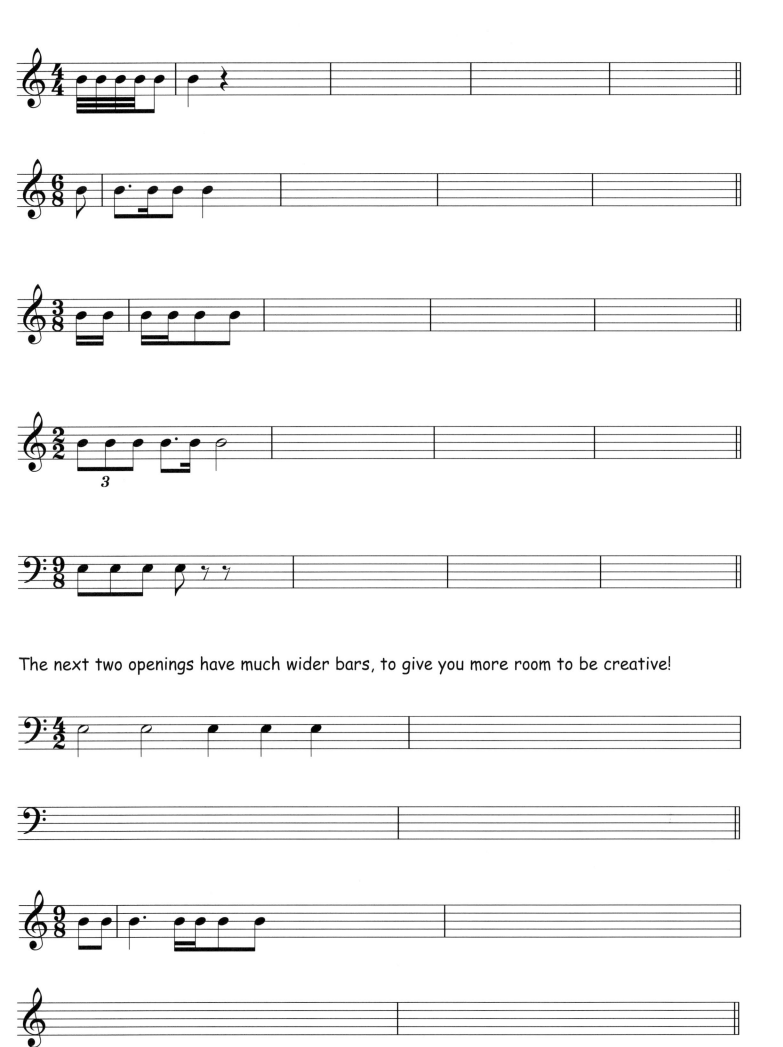

The next two openings have much wider bars, to give you more room to be creative!

Rhythmic Revision

1. Complete these bars with rests in the correct order:

2. Add a time signature to this rhythm:

3. Fill this bar with a single sound (hint: you'll need to use a tie):

4. Circle the time signatures in which we would find a minim rest:

$$\frac{2}{4} \quad \frac{3}{4} \quad \frac{4}{4} \quad \frac{6}{8} \quad \frac{4}{2} \quad \frac{3}{8} \quad \frac{2}{2} \quad \frac{3}{2} \quad \frac{9}{8} \quad \frac{12}{8}$$

5. Fun research: Find out the name for notes with four tails (♪). _____

6. Rewrite this short melody with correct grouping/beaming:

7. Who wrote Chopin's Nocturne in E♭ major? _____ (This should be easy)

8. Write a suitable time signature for compound-triple time. _____

Leger Lines

You are extremely familiar with leger lines by now. All you need to know for Grade 3 is that you may encounter quite a few of them above and below the stave! Name these notes:

_____   _____   _____   _____   _____

Let's revise our old trick of changing clefs to get rid of leger lines. Remember, the pitch of the note should remain the same:

Now for the reverse skill... you'll need lots of leger lines when you rewrite these notes in a different clef!

Very soon (i.e. on the next page) you're going to rewrite melodies in different clefs AND change the pitch of the notes by an octave. Here's an example of how it's done:

Can you rewrite these notes in treble clef AND one octave higher?

Transposition

To transpose a melody is to write the same melody starting on a different note. In Grade 3, you simply have to transpose a melody one octave higher or lower... but you have to CHANGE CLEFS! (ooohhh)

Two things to watch out for when transposing by an octave (lots of people get caught out by these):

1. Make sure you only transpose ONE octave, not two:

2. Make sure you actually DO change the pitch:

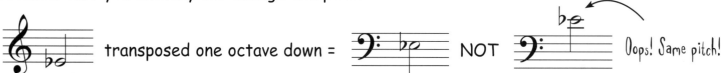

Transposition from one clef to another becomes incredible easy if you picture middle C as an extra line between the treble and bass staves. Transpose these treble notes one octave **lower** into the bass clef. Just count down eight notes!

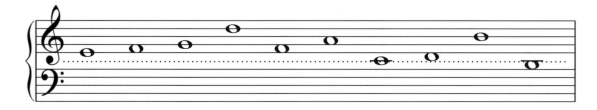

Transpose these notes one octave **higher** into the treble clef: Just count up eight notes!

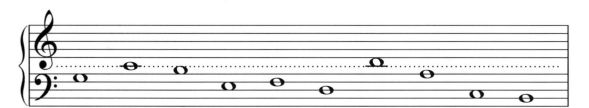

Great work! Now rewrite these notes in a different clef AND transpose them as directed:

octave higher   octave lower   octave higher

Right! Now that you're an expert at transposing single notes up or down an octave, let's do it with an entire melody. Transpose this four-bar melody **one octave lower,** using the bass clef. Spend some time making sure the first note is correct. When writing the rest of the melody, follow the shape and rhythm exactly, and remember to adjust your stems.

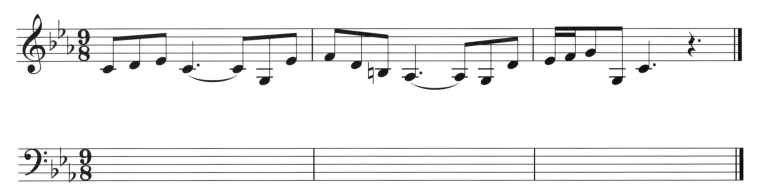

Here's another one... transpose this melody **one octave higher,** using the treble clef.

In what key is the melody you just transposed? _____

And finally, just for fun... transpose your melody ANOTHER octave higher! (Stay in treble clef, obviously.) Write the clef, key signature and time signature.

 HERE'S A THOUGHT... Remember the 'copying' question in Grades 1 and 2? Well, instead of copying the melody exactly, in Grade 3 you may be asked to transpose it up or down an octave, just like you've been doing here. You don't have to worry about including all the dynamics and other details, just the notes. That's good news, huh?!

Rewrite This!

←——————————————→

1. Rewrite this melody with the notes correctly grouped (beamed).

2. Now write your correctly-grouped melody again, this time with notes and rests of TWICE the value. Write the new time signature.

3. Rewrite it AGAIN, keeping your new time signature above... but write it an octave lower, using the bass clef.

4. And, you guessed it, rewrite it one more time, this time with notes TWICE the value again! This means the notes will be QUADRUPLE the value of the original melody! (Wow)

5. True or false: Your final rewrite sounds exactly the same as the original. _____

6. In what key have you written all these melodies? _____

46

Spot the Mistake

In your exam you have to be able to spot the mistakes in the way the music has been written. Sometimes the mistakes are really obvious, sometimes not!

Let's look at a melody that has loads of **obvious** errors in it, like:

★ Clef at incorrect height or missing dots (for bass clef)
★ Accidentals or dots on the wrong side of notes
★ Key signature written incorrectly
★ Stems in wrong direction or on wrong side of note
★ Things being upside down: time signature, expression markings

Find and circle all the mistakes! (There are even some that are not listed above!)

Here is another melody, with **not-so-obvious** mistakes, such as:

★ Wrong time signature or incorrect number of beats in the bar
★ Incorrect grouping
★ Key signature and time signature in wrong order (key signature should go first)
★ Unnecessary ties, or ties and slurs not curving away from the stem

There are just FIVE not-so-obvious mistakes here. Can you circle them?

The next melody contains SIX deliberate mistakes. Rewrite it correctly on the given stave.

Revision of Lots of Things

1. Add time signatures and the missing bar-lines to these melodies.   /8

2. Write a four-bar rhythm using this opening.   /10

3. Name these scales.   /4

_____

_____

_____

_____

4. Which of these time signatures are simple duple? Circle them.   /3

$\frac{2}{4}$ $\frac{3}{4}$ $\frac{6}{8}$ $\frac{4}{4}$ **C** $\frac{3}{8}$ $\frac{2}{2}$ $\frac{3}{2}$ $\frac{9}{8}$ ¢ $\frac{12}{8}$ $\frac{4}{2}$

5. Transpose this melody one octave higher, using the treble clef. /8

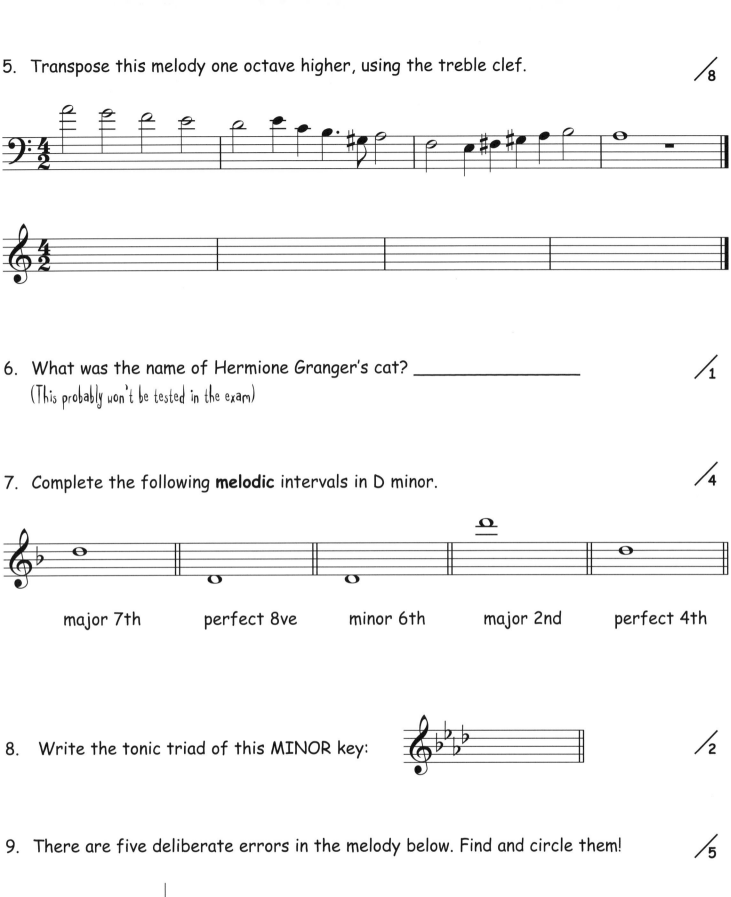

6. What was the name of Hermione Granger's cat? _____ /1
   (This probably won't be tested in the exam)

7. Complete the following **melodic** intervals in D minor. /4

major 7th   perfect 8ve   minor 6th   major 2nd   perfect 4th

8. Write the tonic triad of this MINOR key: /2

9. There are five deliberate errors in the melody below. Find and circle them! /5

Total: /45

Phrasing

A phrase is a musical sentence. The end of a phrase is like a 'breathing point' in the music. In your pieces phrases are shown with long curved lines. However, in your exam, phrases will be marked with square brackets. Here is part of the melody 'Twinkle, Twinkle, Little Star':

etc.

Phrases are usually two, four or eight bars long. The easiest way to getting a feel for the phrasing is to clap the rhythm. Try it for the melody above. Can you mark the remaining two phrases?

Sometimes a phrase begins on an upbeat (anacrusis). This means that most of the other phrases will also begin on an upbeat. Mark the rest of the phrases in 'Happy Birthday' below.

Phrases are not always the same length as each other. A very common structure for phrasing is 2 bars/2 bars/4 bars. Once again, clapping the rhythm gives you a really good feel for this. Can you mark the phrases in this famous melody by Dvořák?

Finally, don't let ties or slurs put you off when marking phrasing. Clap the rhythm of 'The Entertainer' by Scott Joplin, then mark each phrase below with a square bracket.

etc.

Terms and Signs

← →

Once again, there are a whole load of terms to learn for Grade 3, **in addition to** the terms you learned in Grades 1 and 2 (oh well). You can download them all from **www.blitzbooks.com**

adagietto	-	rather slow (not as slow as 'adagio')
ad libitum (ad lib.)	-	play freely
agitato	-	agitated
alla breve (¢)	-	with a minim beat, in $\frac{2}{2}$ (usually faster than $\frac{4}{4}$)
amore/amoroso	-	love/loving
animato	-	animated, lively
ben marcato	-	well marked
comodo	-	convenient/comfortable
con anima	-	with feeling, with spirit
con brio	-	with vigour
con forza	-	with force
deciso	-	with determination
delicato	-	delicately
energico	-	energetically
largamente	-	broadly
leggiero	-	lightly
marziale	-	in a military style
mesto	-	sad
pesante	-	heavy
prima/primo	-	first (e.g. *'prima volta'* = first time)
risoluto	-	bold, resolute
ritmico	-	rhythmically
rubato/tempo rubato	-	with freedom of tempo
scherzando/scherzoso	-	playfully, jokingly
seconda/secondo	-	second
semplice	-	simple
sempre	-	always
stringendo	-	getting faster
subito	-	suddenly
tanto	-	so much
tranquillo	-	calmly
triste/tristamente	-	sadly/sorrowfully

Timed Test

←————————————→

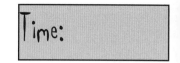

Before you attempt this test, take a few minutes to study page 51. Then, when you're ready, time yourself doing this quiz. Do it as fast as you can, then record your finishing time above. But... guess what? Your teacher will **ADD ON 10 SECONDS** for every mistake you make! It's fun to go fast, but more important to be **accurate**. Start the clock!

1. What does this sign mean? ¢ _____

2. Which is slower, *adagio* or *adagietto*? _____

3. Translate the Italian terms in this sentence: 'The soldiers looked *risoluto* as they took *pesante* steps *marziale*. *Subito* they were *stringendo* as they marched *con forza* towards the barracks!

4. Write two Italian terms that mean 'to play freely' or 'with freedom of tempo'.

    _____ and _____

5. True or false: In duets, the *Primo* part is the second part. _____

6. Which Italian word means the opposite of '*pesante*'? _____

7. What do the words '*triste*' and '*mesto*' have in common? _____

8. What does '*scherzando*' mean? _____

STOP THE CLOCK – FILL IN YOUR TIME AT THE TOP!

After marking this with your teacher, tick one of the following:

☐ I made no mistakes! I keep my time of _____ !

☐ I made _____ mistakes. My new time is _____

Use Your Skills

As you know from previous grades, the final question in your exam paper is centred around a melody, about which you have to answer questions. The next three pages will really prepare you for this! All you need to do is apply all the knowledge and skills you've learned so far in this book.

You'll also be asked to rewrite some or all of the given melody in a different way: halving/doubling the note values, transposing up/down, that kind of thing. Read the question carefully so you know which part to rewrite! You do not have to include the bar numbers or any of the expression markings, just the notes and rests.

Here's your first melody, from a sonatina by Anton Diabelli. Answer the questions below.

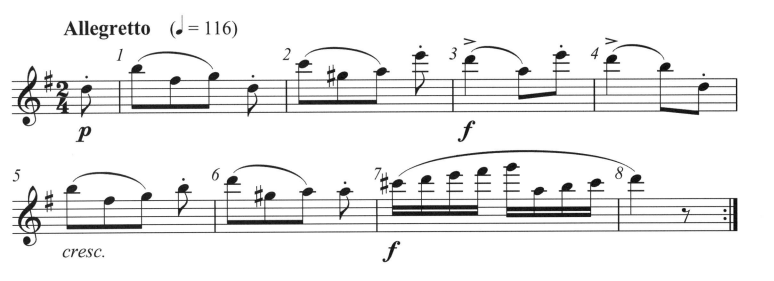

★ At what speed is this music to be played? _____

★ True or false: This melody is in F major. _____

★ Name and explain the sign on each crotchet in bars 3 and 4. _____

★ The key is G major. On which scale degree does the melody end? _____

★ Explain the dots just before the double bar line. _____

★ Why is the last bar missing one quaver beat? _____

★ Which bars contain notes NOT belonging to G major? _____

★ Circle two Italian terms mostly likely to describe the character of this piece.

    Pesante   **Marziale**   **Scherzando**   **Con brio**   **Triste**

Here is the opening of Nocturne in E♭ major by Chopin. Answer the questions below.

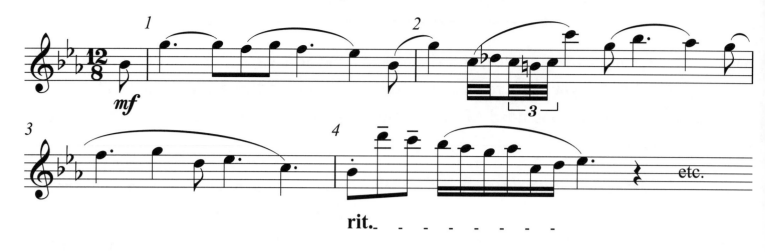

★ How many ties are in this melody? _____ How many slurs? _____

★ In which bar is the performer told to change tempo? _____ Explain the meaning of the Italian term indicating this. _____

★ Explain the '3' under the demisemiquavers in bar 2. _____

★ Underline two words which describe the time signature:

      simple   compound   duple   triple   quadruple

★ Circle the highest note of the melody. Which scale degree is this? _____

★ On the stave below, transpose bars 3 and 4 an octave lower. Do not change the clef.

Here is a melody from a sonatina by Kuhlau. Answer the questions below (and continuing on the next page).

★ What does 'dolce' mean? _____

★ Place square brackets over each of the two phrases.

★ True or false: This melody is in compound-triple time. _____

★ Give the time name of the shortest note in the melody. _____

★ How many WHOLE bars contain semiquavers? _____

★ The melody begins on the tonic note. How many bars contain a note NOT belonging to this key? _____

Here is one last melody to study. It's from the second movement of a sonata by Beethoven.

★ What does ♩ = 56 mean? _____

★ What does 'amoroso' mean? _____

★ Mark the rest of the phrases with square brackets.

★ True or false: This melody is in the key of A major. _____

★ The first note in bar 4 would be equaivalent to _____ demisemiquavers.

★ Who wrote this music? (Come on, this should be easy) _____

★ Circle the Italian word mostly likely to describe the tempo of this piece.

   Largamente   **Sempre**   **Agitato**   **Alla marcia**   **Pasta**

★ On the staves below, rewrite the entire melody an octave lower, using the bass clef.

Just One Last Revision Test (promise!)

1. Rewrite this melody with correct grouping/beaming of the notes: /10

2. Name the key of the melody above: _____ /1

3. Name another key with the same key signature: _____ /1

4. Circle two consecutive notes that make an interval of a major 3rd. /1

5. Rewrite the melody on the stave below, using notes of TWICE the value. /10

6. Above each of the following, write the harmonic interval stated. /5
   The key is F# minor.

       minor 3rd   perfect 5th   major 7th   perfect 8ve   minor 6th

56

7. Add the missing clef, key signature and time signature to this melody in E major. ⁄8
    Then add the missing rest/s at each place marked *.

8. Write a suitable time signature for compound-quadruple time: _____ ⁄1

9. Name two ingredients in chocolate mousse. _____ ⁄2
    (This is not essential Grade 3 knowledge.)

10. Rewrite your answer to question 5 (back on the opposite page) one octave higher, ⁄8
    using the treble clef.

11. Compose a rhythm using this opening. ⁄10

12. Give the English meaning of these terms:

    tempo primo   _____ ⁄3

    alla breve   _____

    semplice   _____

Total: ⁄60

Test Paper... Sort Of

All theory books end with a test paper, but this one is DIFFERENT. It already has the answers in it (mostly wrong answers!) and your job is to be the teacher – you have to **mark** it.

When you've found all the mistakes, go to **www.blitzbooks.com** and download the EXACT SAME PAPER – this time with no answers already in it. See if you can get 100%!

★ ★ ★ ★ ★ ★ ★

Theory Paper Grade 3

TOTAL MARKS
100

Time allowed: 1.5 hours

1   Write the correct time signature for each of these five melodies. They all begin on the first beat of the bar.

10

2 Write a complete four-bar rhythm using the given opening, which begins on an upbeat.

3 This melody contains *five* deliberate mistakes. Rewrite it correctly on the given stave.

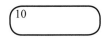

4 Add the correct rest/s at each place marked * to complete the bar.

5 *Above* each of these notes write a *higher* note to form the named harmonic interval. The key is C♯ minor.

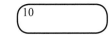

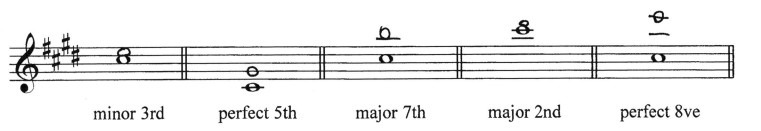

minor 3rd   perfect 5th   major 7th   major 2nd   perfect 8ve

6 Name the key of each of the following scales. Where the key is minor, state whether the scale is harmonic or melodic.

Key .....G harmonic minor....

Key ..C major with a....
....minor 3rd....

Key ....E major........

Key .....E major again....

Key ....F minor........

7 Write the following tonic triads with the correct key signature.

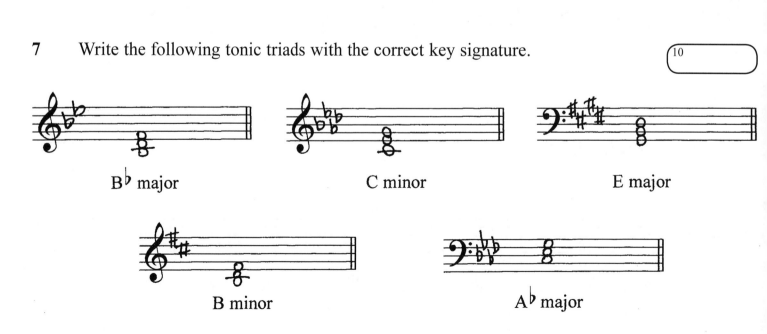

B♭ major   C minor   E major

B minor   A♭ major

Rubato

semplice

a) Give the meaning of:

(i) **Rubato** ...Kind of like free rhythm...

(ii) ◠· (e.g. bars 1, 3, 5 and 7) ...mezzo staccato...

(iii) *semplice* ...simple...

(iv) $\frac{3}{4}$ (give full definition) ...3 beats per bar...

(v) ◠ (e.g. bar 4) ...Semi-circle over a dot...

`10`

b) (i) Which bars contain notes NOT belonging to A major?...3 & 5...

`10`

(ii) Name one similarity and one difference between bars 1, 3, 5 and 7.

Similarity ...They are all odd numbers!...

Difference ...They all start on different notes...

(iii) How many FULL bars contain minims? ...4...

(iv) What is the name of the horizontal line over each minim? ...Tenuto...

(v) The first phrase has been marked with a square bracket. Mark the rest of the phrasing the same way.

c) Rewrite the melody from the beginning to the second beat of bar 4 an octave lower, using the bass clef as shown.

`10`

How did you go marking this paper? Did you find lots of mistakes? Now go to www.blitzbooks.com and download the uncompleted version. Good luck!

Manuscript